CW00594944

Desiree.

Victorian
Britain

Victorian Britain

Photographs by *Andy Williams*
Text by *Nicholas Best*

WEIDENFELD AND NICOLSON
LONDON

INTRODUCTION

*Q*ueen Victoria reigned from 1837 to 1901, monarch of the richest and most powerful nation on earth, monarch also of an empire that embraced one-fifth of the world's population and two-fifths of its land mass. She gave her name to the age, and also to the architecture of the age. It was an architecture that reflected the values of her people - money, power, success - the values of the newly rich who had made a fortune out of the Industrial Revolution and wanted everyone to know it. They built lavish public buildings as well as lavish houses for themselves, decorating every available surface with intricate designs of one kind or another, wanting to show that

they had money and could afford to spend it. They were not aristocrats, with elegant tastes picked up during a grand tour of Europe; they were hard-nosed engineers and industrialists, who had made their cash out of sweat and grime and who wanted to put their wealth where they could see it. It is this fussy, overblown style that people think of as Victorian: the Albert Memorial, say, or St Pancras station. But the truth is that much Victorian building was not Victorian at all in that sense. Lord Palmerston, for instance, was not at all keen on Victorian architecture. He rejected a St Pancras style for the new Foreign Office and chose something Italianate instead. So did Victoria, for her holiday home at Osborne, on the Isle of Wight. So did Morgan Peto, at Somerleyton. Others harked back to the Gothic of an earlier age, or else built themselves neo-Jacobean piles copied entirely from the real thing. They were building in the Victorian era, but they built in all sorts of different styles, as the pictures in this book clearly illustrate.

MONSAL DALE

DERBYSHIRE

*T*HE vast expansion of the railways contributed enormously to the great prosperity of Victorian times. This old viaduct, at Monsal Dale in Derbyshire, was one of many constructed at the height of the railway boom.

HORSE-DRAWN TRAM

CRICH TRAM MUSEUM, DERBYSHIRE

*D*ERBYSHIRE'S Crich museum is devoted entirely to tramcars. The horse-drawn tram on the right was a typical form of transport in Victorian times.

TOWER BRIDGE

LONDON

*T*HE bascules of Tower Bridge swing open to admit the sailing barque 'Marques'. Each bascule weighs 1,000 tons - including its counterweight - and takes 90 seconds to open. The bridge was built in the 1880s.

———•◦•◦•———

CARDIFF CASTLE

SOUTH GLAMORGAN

*T*HERE has been a castle at Cardiff since the 11th century, but much of the present structure dates from the 1860s, when the Marquis of Bute commissioned an elaborate series of reconstructions. The result was Disneyesque, to say the least.

———•—•—

NATURAL HISTORY MUSEUM

LONDON

*I*T is no accident that the Natural History museum in London looks like a cathedral. In the age of Charles Darwin, it was deliberately designed like that as a shrine to the mysteries of the natural world.

BODNANT HALL

GWYNEDD

*B*ODNANT Hall dates from the 1790s but was later much enlarged. The gardens, arguably the most beautiful in Wales, were laid out in the 1870s by Henry Pochin, an industrialist from Lancashire with a great love of trees.

MANCHESTER TOWN HALL

MANCHESTER

*M*ANCHESTER was at the heart of the Industrial Revolution, a city of enormous wealth sitting uneasily alongside great poverty. The town hall, completed in 1876, contains the statues of many important figures, among them Gladstone, Cobden and Bright.

KING'S MILL

*B*UILT in 1879 and still working, this Sussex smock mill once belonged to the writer Hilaire Belloc. He lived in the house nearby for almost 40 years.

FORTH RAIL BRIDGE

BORDERS

$\mathscr{C}$OMPLETED in 1889, the bridge crosses the firth of Forth at the only viable point for 50 miles. It was originally intended to be a suspension bridge, but the design was hastily changed after the collapse of the Tay bridge in 1879.

HOUSES OF PARLIAMENT

LONDON

*T*HE Palace of Westminster, dating from before the Norman conquest, was gutted by fire in 1834. Sir Charles Barry and Augustus Pugin's splendidly Gothic Parliament buildings replaced it in 1840.

ROYAL EXCHANGE

LONDON

*T*HE exchange, originally a place where merchants did business, sits at the heart of the City of London, with the Bank of England on the left. The present building replaced the earlier exchange, burned down in 1838.

OSBORNE

ISLE OF WIGHT

*D*ESIGNED as a holiday home for Victoria and Albert, Osborne, on the Isle of Wight, was the favourite of all their houses. Because of its happy memories, Victoria spent as much time as she could there after Albert's death. She herself died at Osborne in 1901.

ASTOR ESTATE HOUSE

LONDON

*T*HIS grand-looking house in London's Temple Place was built in 1895. It used to belong to the Astor family and Lord Astor ran his numerous business affairs from here.

----•••----

SOMERLEYTON HALL

SUFFOLK

*I*N 1844 the previous house on the site was bought by Morgan Peto, a former bricklayer who had made a fortune as a railway contractor. He intended to transform it into a 'Jacobean' mansion, but with an Italian tower at one end and pale French stone throughout, he created something else entirely.

LAW COURTS

LONDON

*T*HE style is 13th century, but the Royal Courts of Justice in London's Strand were actually designed in 1874. Many of the country's most notorious trials have been held here.

ALBERT MEMORIAL

LONDON

*G*ROTESQUE to some, a delight to others, the memorial in Kensington Gardens shows Prince Albert holding a catalogue of the Great Exhibition of 1851.

ALBERT HALL

LONDON

*N*AMED after Victoria's husband, the hall can hold up to 8,000 people for a concert. Its roof was a minor miracle of engineering in its day. When the last of the scaffolding was removed, no one knew for sure whether it would collapse or not.

WADDESDON MANOR

BUCKINGHAMSHIRE

*I*T looks Renaissance in style, but the house was built between 1874 and 1889 by Baron de Rothschild, a highly cultivated man who loved everything French, particularly the architecture.

ST PANCRAS STATION

LONDON

*D*ESIGNED as a showcase for the Midland Railway, the Grand Midland Hotel at London's St Pancras station is arguably the single most distinguished building of the 19th century Gothic revival.

ALBERT BRIDGE

LONDON

*S*PANNING the Thames at Chelsea, where Sir Thomas More had his country home, the bridge sparkles against the sunset. Notices at both ends of it require troops to break step when marching across.

THORESBY HALL

NOTTINGHAM

*T*HE design of the hall is comparatively restrained, by Victorian standards. It sits in the middle of Sherwood forest, with 29 rooms on the main floor and a total of 78 bedrooms.

———•◦•◦•———

OLD BAILEY

LONDON

*B*LIND and impartial, the statue of justice stands above the Central Criminal Court, built on the site of London's Newgate prison. The street outside – Old Bailey – is wider than most, to accommodate the crowds at public hangings.

SANDRINGHAM HOUSE

NORFOLK

*S*OLIDLY neo-Jacobean in style, the house was built for the future Edward VII in 1870 and still belongs to the Royal family. The estate has one of the best pheasant shoots in the country.

OLD CURIOSITY SHOP

LONDON

*E*XPERTS disagree as to whether this really was the inspiration for Dickens' shop. It dates from the 17th century however, so it was certainly a familiar sight in Little Nell's time.

———•••———

ACKNOWLEDGEMENTS

Text © Weidenfeld & Nicolson 1995
Photographs © Andy Williams

First published in Great Britain in 1995 by George Weidenfeld & Nicolson Ltd
Orion House, 5 Upper St Martin's Lane, London WC2H 9EA

British Library Cataloguing-in-Publication Data
A catalogue record for this book is available from the British Library

Cover and series design by Peter Bridgewater/Bridgewater Book Company
House Editor: Beth Vaughan

Front cover: The Palm House, Kew Gardens
Half-title illustration: Natural History Museum, London
Frontispiece: Liver Building, Liverpool
Introduction: White Tower Cardiff Castle, South Wales